WHY DO I GET A TOOTHACHE?

✦ and other questions about nerves ✦

Angela Royston

Heinemann Library
Chicago, Illinois

© 2003 Reed Educational & Professional Publishing
Published by Heinemann Library,
an imprint of Reed Educational & Professional Publishing,
Chicago, Illinois

Customer Service 888-454-2279
Visit our website at www.heinemannlibrary.com

Designed by Joanna Sapwell and StoryBooks
Illustrations by Nick Hawken
Originated by Ambassador Litho
Printed by South China Printers, Hong Kong

07 06 05 04 03
10 9 8 7 6 5 4 3 2 1

Library of Congress Cataloging-in-Publication Data
Royston, Angela.
Why do I get a toothache? : and other questions about nerves / Angela Royston.
     p. cm. -- (Body matters)
Includes index.
Summary: Answers common questions about the nervous system.
  ISBN 1-40340-204-3 (HC)   ISBN 1-40340-459-3 (PB)
  1. Nervous system--Juvenile literature. [1. Nervous system.] I.
Title. II. Series.
  QP361.5 .R693 2002
  612.8--dc21
                              2002003545

Acknowledgments
The author and publishers are grateful to the following for permission to reproduce copyright material:
pp. 4, 6, 7, 10, 12, 16, 24, 28 Science Photo Library; pp. 5, 14, 18, 20, 23 Gareth Boden; p. 9 Robert Harding; pp. 13, 27 Powerstock/Zefa; p. 19 Eyewire.

Cover photograph by Gareth Boden.

Some words are shown in bold, **like this.** You can find out what they mean by looking in the glossary.

CONTENTS

WHAT ARE NERVES?

Nerves are like the body's telephone system. They carry electrical signals to and from the brain. There are two kinds of nerves, **sensory nerves** and **motor nerves.** Sensory nerves connect your eyes, ears, skin, mouth, and nose with your brain. The signals they carry give your brain information about what is happening in the world outside. Motor nerves carry signals from your brain to your muscles to make them work.

The senses

You have five senses—sight, hearing, taste, smell, and touch. Each sense has its own sense **organ** or organs. These are the eyes, the ears, the tongue, the nose, and the skin. Sense organs have nerve endings that react to different kinds of things, such as light, heat, or chemicals.

In a nerve cell, the dendrites pick up electrical signals from another nerve cell and pass them along the axon to the nerve endings. The nucleus controls the cell.

dendrites   nucleus   axon

4

Chemicals in your food **trigger** your sense of taste, and nerve endings in your nose react to chemicals in the air so you can smell.

Carrying the message

When the nerve endings are exposed to the right kind of trigger, they send electrical signals to the brain. The signals travel along a fine nerve fiber. Nerve fibers join together to make a chain of communication to the brain. The brain itself is a mass of interconnecting nerve **cells.** It can send electrical signals along the motor nerves to the muscles.

This girl's brain is receiving messages from several sense organs. She is listening to music through her headphones while seeing, touching, and tasting the orange.

THE SENSES

Sense	Sense organ	Reacts to
Sight	Eyes	Light
Hearing	Ears	Sound
Touch	Skin	Touch, heat, and cold
Taste	Mouth	Chemicals
Smell	Nose	Chemicals

WHY CAN'T I SEE IN THE DARK?

The nerve endings inside your eyes react to light. If you cover your eyes, you will not see anything because no light can reach your eyes. It is dark outside at night, but there is usually some light—from street lights, the moon, and the stars. Your eyes react to this light but you still cannot see clearly. This is because only some of the nerve endings can detect dim light.

You cannot see clearly in dim light and at night. One thing merges into another and everything looks gray, black, or white.

The retina

The **retina** is a kind of screen inside the back of the eye. It contains two kinds of nerve endings that react to light. They are called rods and cones. Rods react to light and dark, and see things in shades of gray. Cones need a lot of light but they can see color. During the day the nerve endings in the retina absorb light and react to different colors, but at night they can only see shapes in black and white.

Optic nerve

Nerve fibers from each rod and cone join together to make the **optic nerve.** It collects signals for all the rods and cones and carries them to the brain.

RODS AND CONES

You have about 126 million nerve endings in the retina of each eye. About 120 million of them are rods and about 6 million are cones. Most of the cones are concentrated in a small patch in the center of the retina.

This is what the retina looks like. It is packed with nerve endings that react to weak and strong light.

HOW DOES MY EYE WORK?

Each eye works like a camera. When you look in a mirror you can see a black circle in the middle of each eye. This is an opening called the pupil. Light bounces off objects in front of you and passes through the pupil into your eye. Just inside the eye is a lens. The lens bends the light so that it makes a clear picture on the **retina,** but the picture it makes is upside-down. The nerve endings in the retina send the picture to the brain as electrical signals. You do not see everything upside-down because the brain turns the picture the right way up.

The part of the eye that you see in the mirror is only a small part of the whole eye. The rest is hidden inside your head.

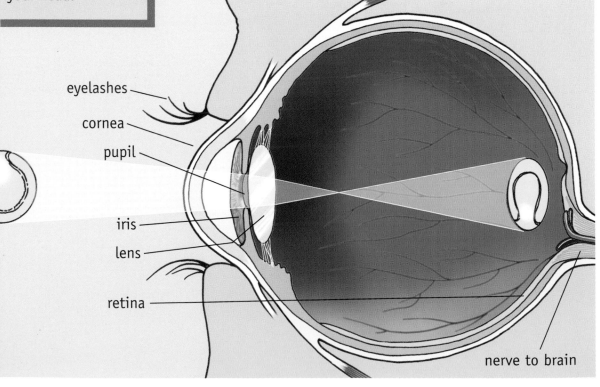

eyelashes

cornea

pupil

iris

lens

retina

nerve to brain

The iris

The iris is the colored ring around the pupil. It contains two circles of muscles that control the amount of light that enters the eye. When bright light hits the iris, nerves tell one of the circles of muscle to close the pupil and make it smaller. This stops too much light from entering the eye and damaging the retina. In dim light, nerve signals trigger the other circle of muscle to open the pupil to let more light in.

Protecting the eye

The front of the eye is protected by a see-through covering, called the cornea, and by tears, the salty water in your eye. Every time you blink, the eyelid washes the cornea with liquid, like a windshield wiper. The water and cornea stop dirt and germs from getting inside the eye. When a speck of dust or something larger comes close to your eye, nerves trigger your eyelid to blink automatically and protect your eye.

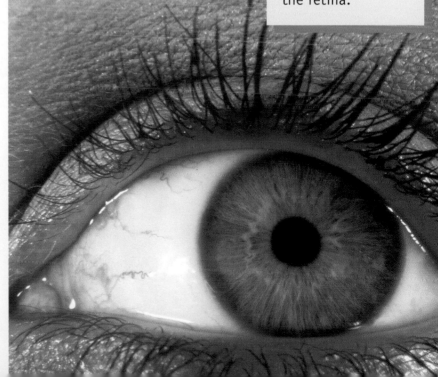

Very bright light can damage the nerve endings in the retina. The iris opens and closes to control the amount of light that reaches the retina.

WHY DO LOUD NOISES HURT MY EARS?

Very loud noises can damage the nerve endings deep within your ears. The pain acts as a warning so that you can protect your ears from the sound. Even if loud noises do not cause you pain, they can still damage the nerve endings and make them less sensitive to sounds. Listening to loud music over a period of time can cause deafness that only becomes apparent several years later.

People who work with loud sounds, such as the noise made by this chainsaw, cover their ears with ear protectors.

Hearing

Sound is produced by vibrations. A drum, for example, vibrates when it is hit and makes the air around it vibrate too. The vibrations ripple through the air. Some of them reach your ears and travel down the ear canal. The vibrations are passed through your ear to the eardrum and the tiny bones of the middle ear to the inner ear.

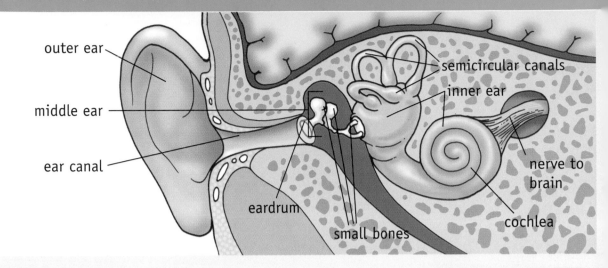

outer ear

semicircular canals

inner ear

middle ear

ear canal

nerve to brain

eardrum

small bones

cochlea

The inner ear

The inner ear is filled with liquid and consists of two different parts—the cochlea and the **semicircular canals.** The cochlea contains the nerve endings that react to sound vibrations. The liquid inside the cochlea vibrates and moves millions of tiny hairs. Each hair is attached to a nerve ending that then sends electrical signals along the auditory nerve, the nerve that takes the signals to the brain.

Sound travels through air, solid bone, and liquid before it reaches the nerve endings in the inner ear.

WHAT MAKES MY EARS POP?

When you take off or land in an airplane, your ears may "pop." Sounds become muffled because the air pressure on one side of the eardrum is greater than on the other side. When the pressure becomes equal again, your ears "pop" back to normal.

WHY DOES SPINNING MAKE ME DIZZY?

When you spin around you quickly become dizzy—although you stand still the world seems to spin. Your sense of balance is confused. The **semicircular canals** in your inner ear help to control your sense of balance. Every time you move your head, the liquid inside them moves and nerve endings send signals to your brain. When you spin around and then stop, the liquid continues to move for a time, so that your brain thinks that you are still spinning. This is what causes you to feel dizzy.

Nerve cells for balance are in the inner ear. When you move your head, liquid inside the semicircular canals **triggers** them.

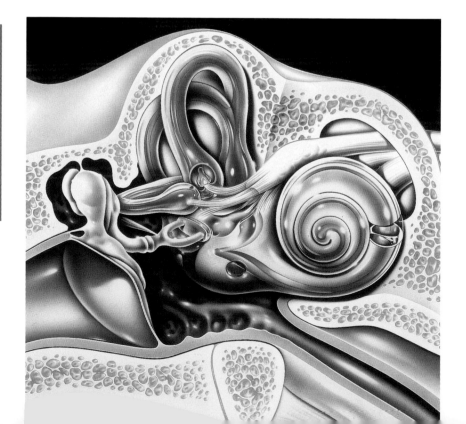

Sense of balance

The three semicircular canals are at right angles to each other. This means that they can sense every movement, whatever direction it is in. If you lean too far in one direction, for example, your brain realizes that you are about to fall over. This allows you to correct your position.

Perfect balance

The semicircular canals can detect even the slightest movement. Some people have trained themselves to be aware of these tiny movements. Acrobats, ballerinas, and gymnasts have such a well-developed sense of balance they can, for example, walk along a wire, balance on tiptoe, or do a somersault on a beam.

Spinning without becoming dizzy

Ballet dancers use a special technique that allows them to spin on the spot without becoming dizzy. They stare at a spot straight ahead of them as they turn their body. Then they turn their head to look again at the same spot as their body goes on turning. This stops the liquid in the semicircular canals from moving out of control.

You need a good sense of balance to inline skate. The more you practice, the better you will become.

WHY CAN'T I SMELL WHEN I HAVE A COLD?

Some smells are much more pleasant than others. Flowers produce a sweet smell to attract bees and insects to them, but we like their smell too.

The nerve endings that produce your sense of smell are at the very top of the inside of your nose. When you have a cold, your nose becomes filled with **mucus.** The mucus prevents the chemicals from reaching the nerve endings at the top of your nose, so you do not smell anything.

Scents and smells

Smells come from **molecules** of gas. Molecules escape most easily from things that smell the most. The liquid in a bottle of perfume, for example, changes easily into gas, and heavily scented flowers release molecules that smell. Substances such as stone do not release molecules, so they do not smell.

Chemicals in the nose

Molecules drift through the air and enter your nose when you breathe in. They **dissolve** in the mucus that covers the nerve endings that produce the sense of smell.

The nerves then carry signals to your brain. If you want to smell something better, you sniff hard. This pulls more molecules up to the top of your nose.

Telling one smell from another

Scientists do not know how the brain tells one smell from another, but some people are better at detecting and identifying smells than other people. They probably pay more attention to smells and learn to distinguish them. Blind people, for example, who cannot rely on their sense of sight, are often much more aware of smells than sighted people. Chemists who work in the perfume industry also have a well-developed sense of smell.

Nerve endings at the top of the nose react to chemicals in the air to produce the sense of smell.

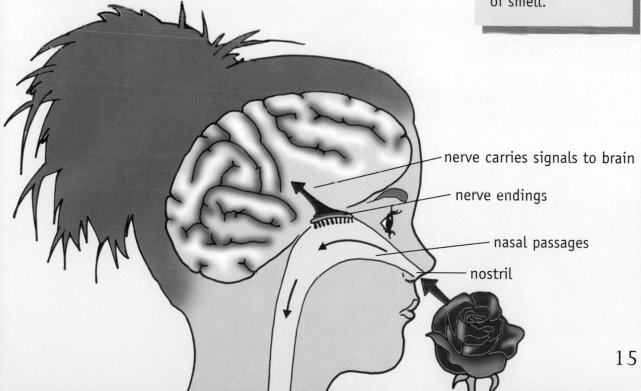

nerve carries signals to brain

nerve endings

nasal passages

nostril

WHY DO SOME THINGS TASTE NASTY?

Some things taste nasty to stop you from eating them. Food that has begun to rot smells and tastes nasty. Many poisons taste very bitter and make you automatically spit them out. But many things that are harmless do not taste nice. People vary in what they like to eat—some people like the taste of spinach, for example, but others think it is disgusting.

Round taste buds on the tongue contain nerve endings that react to ingredients in food and produce the sense of taste.

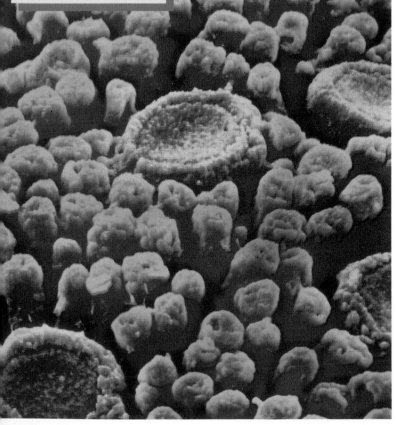

Taste buds

The nerve endings that produce the sense of taste are hidden in small mounds, called taste buds. Most of them are on your tongue but some are in other parts of the mouth. Chemicals in the food or drink **dissolve** in saliva and this trickles through the taste bud to the nerve endings. You cannot taste very well if your mouth is dry.

Different tastes

Scientists think that taste buds can detect only four kinds of taste— sweet, bitter, salty, and sour. Every taste is made up of a different combination of these four. A chocolate bar, for example, contains some cocoa, which is very bitter, and plenty of sugar, which is sweet. Most people prefer sweet and salty tastes and think that very bitter or sour tastes are nasty. Coffee tastes bitter, while vinegar and lemon juice taste sour.

TASTE AND SMELL

Taste and smell work together. Much of what you experience as taste is probably smell. Test yourself by blocking your nose and blindfolding your eyes. You will then find it much harder to identify tastes.

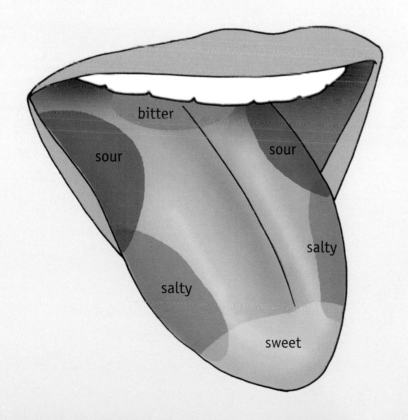

bitter

sour

sour

salty

salty

sweet

The tongue contains about 3,000 taste buds. Different parts of the tongue have taste buds that react mainly to one kind of taste.

17

WHY DO I FEEL PAIN?

If you grab a thorn you will feel a sharp pain. This makes you let go before it injures you further.

We feel pain when particular nerve endings are **triggered.** These nerve endings are in almost every part of the body and they are usually triggered by an injury or by illness. A heavy blow, for example, will trigger pain in your skin and muscles. Depending on where it falls, it may cause bleeding inside your body that leads to bruises or damage to your internal **organs.** A sore throat is often the first sign of a cold. The cold germs attack the throat and make it red and sore.

Inflammation

If you sprain your ankle, the tendons or ligaments around the joint may be damaged. The ankle becomes swollen with extra liquid that forms a cushion around the joint to protect it from further damage. The fact that your ankle is painful stops you from using it, so the pain protects it from further stresses and strains while the damage heals.

The sling will keep this boy from moving his sprained wrist while it is sore. A bandage will help support the joint while it heals.

Pain is a warning

Pain is unpleasant but it is also useful because it tells you that there is something wrong. The pain in a sprained wrist stops you from using it and damaging the joint further. A headache tells you that you may be getting sick and need to rest. If you never felt pain, you might not know when you had hurt yourself or were ill.

DESCRIBING PAIN

There are many different kinds of pain. These are some words that can be used to describe pain:

twinge	dull ache
smarting	stinging
throbbing	sharp
stabbing	agony

WHY DO I GET A TOOTHACHE?

You get a toothache when something **triggers** the nerve endings deep within the tooth. The outside of each tooth is covered with enamel, a very hard substance that contains no nerves. Underneath the enamel is dentine, which is as hard as bone, but in the middle of each tooth is a soft pulp that contains blood and nerves. If you eat something very cold, such as ice cream, the cold may travel through your tooth and trigger the nerve endings. Tooth decay causes a much more serious toothache.

A toothache caused by tooth decay can be painful. If your tooth aches you should see a dentist right away.

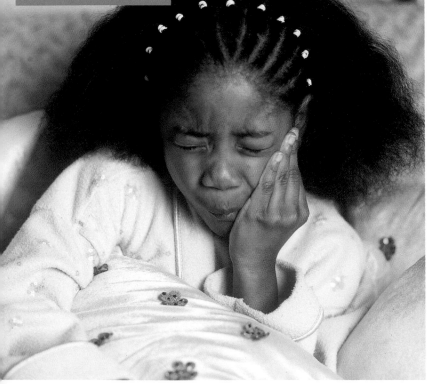

Tooth decay

Bacteria in your mouth feed on pieces of food that cling in saliva around your teeth. They produce a strong acid that gradually wears down the enamel and makes a hole in the dentine. If the decay is not stopped by a dentist the hole will eventually reach the nerve endings in the middle of the tooth. They will send powerful signals to your brain that you will experience as an agonizing toothache. Brushing your teeth and having them checked regularly by a dentist will stop tooth decay before it causes a toothache.

Sense of touch

The nerve endings that react to pain and to cold are part of the sense of touch. This sense tells you how things feel. Most of the nerve endings that give you a sense of touch are in the skin. Some parts of the skin contain more nerve endings than other parts and so they are more sensitive. The inside of each tooth is very sensitive too.

Different nerve endings in your skin react to pain, heat, cold, touch, and pressure. The pulp in the middle of each tooth contains lots of nerve endings that react to pain.

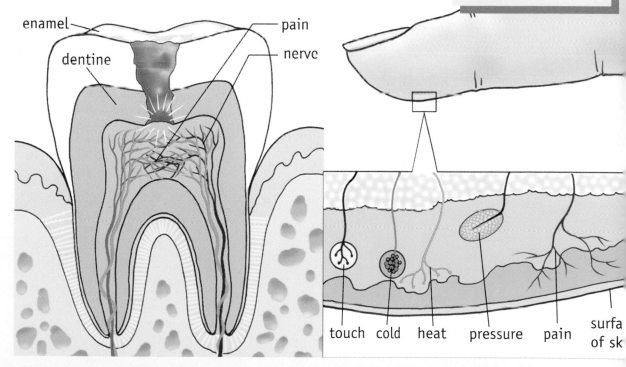

enamel — pain

dentine — nerve

touch   cold   heat   pressure   pain   surfa of sk

21

WHAT IS A REFLEX ACTION?

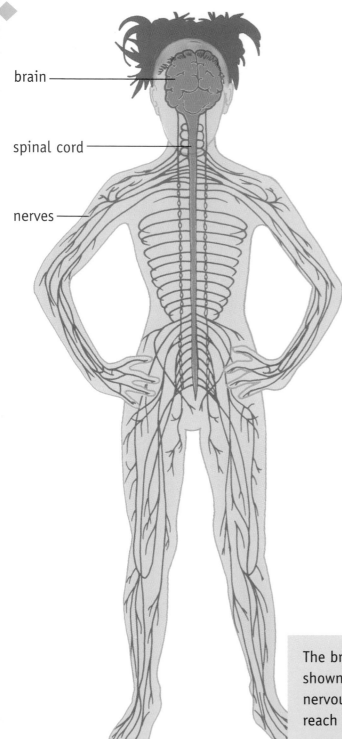

brain

spinal cord

nerves

If you touch something that is hot, you instantly pull your hand away. This is a reflex action. You do it without thinking and it may even take a few seconds before you feel the pain. Usually **sensory nerves** send messages to the brain and this makes you aware of what is happening. The brain then sends messages along the **motor nerves** to your muscles to make them act. But in an emergency, the body takes action before the messages have even reached the brain. It can do this because the link between the sensory and motor nerves is made in the spinal cord.

The brain and the spinal cord, shown in red, form the central nervous system. Its nerves reach all over the body.

Spinal cord

The spinal cord is a bundle of nerves that runs down the middle of your spine. It carries sensory nerves and motor nerves that connect your brain with every part of your body except your eyes, ears, mouth, nose, neck, and vital organs, such as your heart. Twelve pairs of nerves connect these parts directly with the brain. The spinal cord carries 31 pairs of nerves that branch out from it to your arms, back, chest, abdomen, and legs.

Short cut

The signals that make your muscles work are carried by motor nerves. They usually come from the brain but the spinal cord contains special nerves called **relay nerves.** In a reflex action, signals from the sensory nerves pass through the relay nerve directly to the motor nerve. The muscles then react before you are aware that anything has happened.

As the boy's foot touches the thumbtack, he jerks it away in a reflex action. A relay nerve passes the message from the sensory nerves on his foot to his leg muscles.

WHAT DOES MY BRAIN DO?

Your brain controls your body. It receives information about the world through the sense **organs,** analyzes it, and then sends messages to your muscles to take action. It also controls your heart, stomach, and other vital organs and systems that keep you alive. All your thoughts, feelings, and actions are formed in the brain.

What is the brain?

The brain is a soft grayish-pink lump that looks like a huge walnut. It rests in your head behind your eyes and forehead and is protected by the skull. The brain consists mainly of billions of nerve **cells** that link together to form a complex system of interconnected networks. The brain has three main parts—the **cerebrum,** the **cerebellum,** and the **brain stem.**

Billions of nerve cells make up the brain. Each nerve cell may be linked to as many as 50,000 other cells. They form a powerful network.

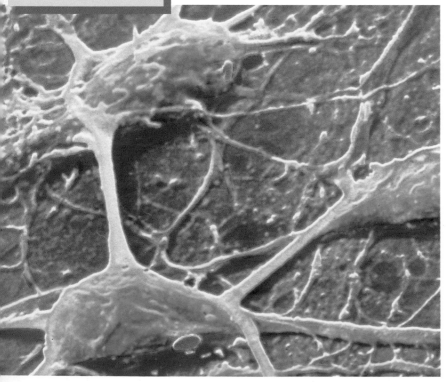

Cerebrum

The cerebrum takes up more than four-fifths of the brain and is responsible for everything that you are aware of, such as seeing, hearing, feeling, planning, and moving. The outer layer of the cerebrum is called the cortex. Different areas of it deal with different things. The area at the front, for example, deals with thinking and planning, while the area that deals with seeing is at the back. A strip across the middle takes in signals from the sense of touch. It lies next to a strip that sends messages to the **motor nerves** in different parts of the body. Parts of the body that are sensitive or that you use a lot, such as your hands and lips, take up larger areas on these strips than, say, your back.

The cortex controls the thoughts, sensations, and actions that you are aware of. Different areas of it deal with different things.

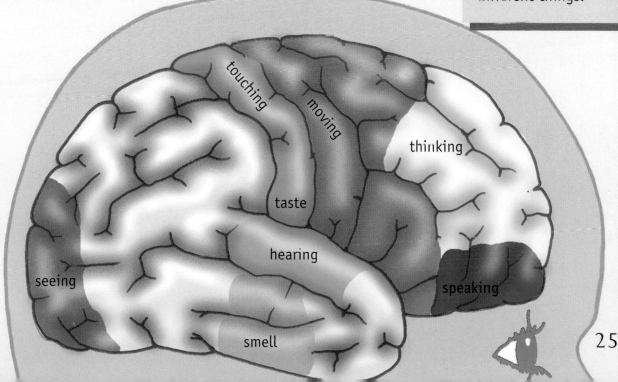

touching

moving

thinking

taste

hearing

seeing

speaking

smell

Cerebellum

The **cerebellum** lies below the **cerebrum.** When the cerebrum sends out signals to the muscles to perform a particular action, the cerebellum coordinates the signals with the action to make sure that your body moves smoothly. The cerebellum also plays an important role in the sense of balance.

Brain stem

The **brain stem** controls the **organs** and systems inside your body that keep you alive. It keeps your heart beating, your blood flowing, your lungs taking in and expelling air, and your stomach and intestines digesting food.

This is what the brain would look like if you sliced through it. Below the cerebrum are the cerebellum and the brain stem.

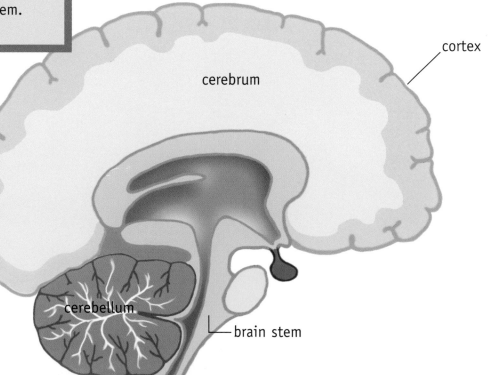

cortex

cerebrum

cerebellum

brain stem

One part of the brain stem makes sure that your body stays at the right temperature. When you are hot, it makes your skin sweat to cool you down. It also controls the amount of water in your body. When you need to take in more water, it makes you feel thirsty.

Working unaware

Most of the nerves that link the heart, liver, kidneys, and other organs to the brain do not pass through the cortex, so you are not usually aware of these parts of your body. You only become aware of your stomach, for example, when you feel hungry or when something goes wrong and your stomach aches.

Sleep

When you fall asleep, most of the cerebrum closes down, but the rest of the brain goes on working. While you are asleep you probably dream up to about five times a night, but you are usually only aware of a dream if you wake up in the middle of it.

This athlete is hot and thirsty. The brain stem controls temperature and water balance to keep the body's internal environment steady.

Studying the brain

Scientists study the brain in several ways. An electroencephalograph is a machine that measures and records electrical activity in the brain. Scientists use it to study sleep and dreams. A PET (positron emission tomography) scan shows which parts of the brain are working when someone does a particular activity, such as writing or listening to music. When part of the brain is damaged, scientists can see which part of the body is affected.

Psychology

Psychologists study how people behave. For example, they look at how people remember things and how they learn. They may try to find out why some people are more violent than others. There is much about the brain that scientists still do not understand.

The red areas on this PET scan show which parts of the brain are being used.

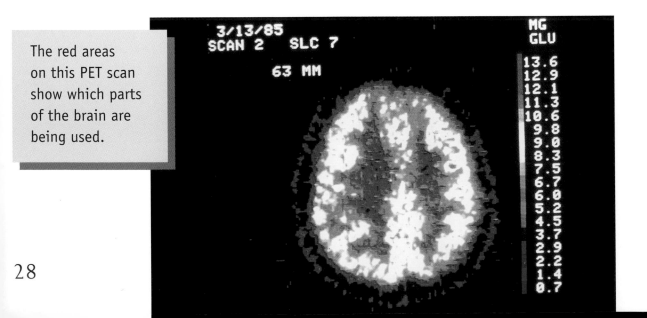

BODY MAP

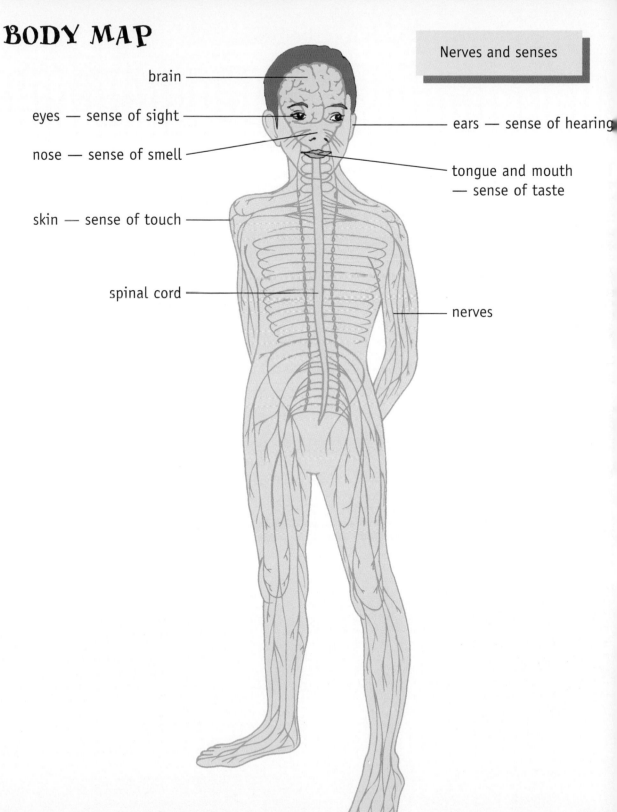

Nerves and senses

brain

eyes — sense of sight

nose — sense of smell

skin — sense of touch

spinal cord

ears — sense of hearing

tongue and mouth
— sense of taste

nerves

GLOSSARY

brain stem   part of the brain that controls the organs without you being aware of it

cell   smallest building block of living things. The body has many kinds of cells, including bone cells, muscle cells, and blood cells.

cerebellum   part of the brain that coordinates signals to the motor nerves so that your body moves smoothly

cerebrum   part of the brain that is responsible for everything you are aware of

dissolve   to mix a solid and a liquid so that the solid seems to disappear into the liquid. For example when you mix salt into water, the salt seems to disappear.

molecule   smallest particle into which a substance can be divided and still be the substance

motor nerve   nerve that carries electrical signals from the brain to a muscle

mucus   slimy liquid produced by the lining of the nose, bronchial tubes, and other parts of the body

optic nerve   nerve that takes electrical signals from the nerve endings in the retina to the brain

organ part of the body, for example the heart, that carries out a particular process

relay nerve nerve in the spinal cord that passes electrical signals from a sensory nerve directly to a motor nerve, bypassing the brain

retina screen at the back of the inside of the eye that reacts to light

semicircular canals three tubes in the inner ear that relay information about balance and movement to the brain

sensory nerve nerve that carries electrical signals from the sense organs to the brain

trigger make something happen

FURTHER READING

Llamas, Andrew. *The Nervous System*. Milwaukee, Wis.: Gareth Stevens, 1998.

Royston, Angela. *Thinking and Feeling*. Chicago: Heinemann Library, 1997.

Stille, Darlene. *Nervous System*. Danbury, Conn.: Children's Press, 1998.

INDEX